Christian
Poems and Plays

D1729759

Grenita Hall

ISBN: 978-955312-00-4

Printed in the United States of America
Story Corner Publishing & Consulting, Inc.
1510 Atlanta Ave.
Portsmouth, VA 23704

Storycornerpublishing@yahoo.com
www.StoryCornerPublishing.com

BOOK OF CONTENT

DEDICATION

This book is dedicated to those that are not here to celebrate this great journey God has me on. I am just so honored that God would choose to use me to touch His people. I want to give a special thanks to Mollie Smith, Willie Smith, Willie Mae Smith & Ella Jean Smith, Tryphenia Toliver, Raymond Toliver, Joe Pope, Robert Lee Smith for being my motivation.

Let Jesus Set You Up

Let Jesus set you up.
Don't get set up by the devil; his plans are tricky and not good at all.
Why take the fall for the devil at all?
Jesus is King, son of the true and living GOD.
Knowing Jesus is better than silver and gold.
Let Him direct your footsteps and allow Him take control.
You may say, "I don't understand The Master's plans."
Just give Jesus a chance because He has plans of good and not evil for us.
We put our hope in all the wrong things for all the wrong reasons.
We do this too often.
We dance to the beat of the devil.
We give Him all the praise.
Then we call on the Father when things do not go as planned.
Oh GOD, yes!
That's what we do.
Stop playing games and give Jesus your life.
Let Jesus set you up.

THE HOSPITAL OF RENEWAL

Have you gotten your check up yet?

Well, if not, GOD is waiting for you to come into the house of the Lord.

Let GOD heal your mind, check your eyes, check your heart, and flush it out.

Allow Him to renew your soul so you can walk bold in purpose.

This hospital is not just for those that is already saved, but for all.

This hospital is for you as well.

GOD will accept you right where you stand, so jump on board today.

Don't be ashamed.

Don't be shy.

Stop telling yourself the same old lie.

The lie that you are ok, or you have arrived.

Let GOD help you and feed you His Word.

Amen?

Can't live by bread alone,

But by every word that preceded out of the mouth of God.

When that fear set in surrender it to GOD.

He will step in and protect us.

When that fear set in,

GOD will be that friend that will be with you all the way.

You will never have to go astray ever again!

The hospital of renewal is truly our friend.

MY LIFE IS LIKE A CHAPTER

My life is a chapter story.
After the story, what does life even mean at all?
One minute you are up and the next you are down.
Feeling like a roller coaster hitting and bumping into wall after wall.
Everything has slipped through my fingers.
Like a rose, we watch it grow.
You turn away for a second, then it's gone!
Not even a shadow or a trace.
It slipped by like the sand on a beach.
I then discover a soft breeze that flows like the river.
I realize that breeze is JESUS.
I feel we sometimes fail GOD or ourselves.
Then that breeze that blew by,
Returns to let me know I am on the right track.
In that breeze, Jesus also let me know I am truly His friend.
Get ready for the next level.
It's coming again.
Stand strong!
I have you and all that is dear and connected to you.
So, no worries or fear.
I'm standing right here He whispers.

STOP BEING A PROBLEM SOLVER

We as GOD's people are always trying to solve our own problems.
This is not Jeopardy or The Price Is Right.
It is not even Family Feud.
Stop trying to solve the puzzle for a prize.
Stop going on a quest to solve problems.
By trying to read their mind or hearing half a story,
We give others information that we ourselves would not even follow.
You know it is misleading and far from the truth.
GOD solves our problems.
He knows each situation from the beginning to the end.
Put your trust in a true friend and believe to the end.
Why not trust GOD?
He has the solution to all your troubles.
That sounds good, I know.
That just burst your bubble of thinking you know it all.
So, let's go and make GOD your problem solver right now.

FLYING ON THE WINGS OF GOD

When our lives seem to be a mess, hold on to the wings of GOD.
Yes, we go through the storms.
The test may be hard but hold on to the wings of GOD.
There is nothing GOD can't do.
Hold on to the wings of GOD.
In His wings there is protection and provision.
We find ourselves sitting in darkness at times
Then the light of JESUS comes right in.
So, jump for joy and jump on the amazing wings of GOD.
The wings of peace, love, patients, faith, and forgiveness,
GOD can heal you.
He can do anything.
Hold on to GOD's beautiful wings.
There is no price to pay because JESUS paved the way.
This walk is free of charge,
So, hold on to the holy wings of GOD as I do every day.

HEAVEN IS MY HOME

Heaven is my home.
Yes, heaven is my home because my Father told me so.
There are many mansions there and one has my name on it.
The streets are made of gold.
The gates are giant pearls.
The light there is like precious stones.
There shall be no night.
The trees are as green as the wonderful grass.
Heaven is filled with peace, joy, and praise.
This vision sound unbelievable, but it is real!
My father told me so crystal clear.
Milk like honey, Oh GOD thank you heaven is truly my home.
It's greater than money!
I am praising and shouting all day long because heaven is my home.
No sleeping there.
Just singing and praising all day long because heaven is my home.
Yes, I claimed heaven.
It's truly my home Father.
GOD I will one day be with you.
Heaven is my home.

WHAT KIND OF THINGS CAN GOD DO?

GOD makes the rain come down to wet the land.

GOD makes the sun to shine to brighten up my day.

GOD keeps His hands on me to protect me everywhere I go.

GOD keeps food on my table and clothes on my back.

I lack nothing good because that is the kind of GOD I serve.

GOD speaks through me.

His Holy Spirit keeps me in his loving word to direct my footsteps in the right path.

I know, GOD is truly who He say He is because He is with me every day.

He allows you and I to live despite our faults.

He gives us chances to get things right.

What kind of things can GOD do?

He can do all things because there is nothing impossible for GOD.

EVEN WHEN MY EYES ARE COVERED, I SEE

Even in darkness, the light will creep in unexpectedly through pain.

Going through and crying out only to see the devil on my trail.

He only comes to steal, kill, and destroy.

Of course, he doesn't want me to see the power of GOD through receiving GOD's Word.

The devil wants me to be distracted.

He uses a veil to cover my eyes after fear has entered in my heart.

I'm tired of running Lord.

I see even when my hands are covering my eyes.

GOD, you still allow me to see sin for what it is even when it is near.

The presence of your Holy Spirit keeps me.

You allowed the light to come in and take over the darkness.

I see GOD while my hands are covering my eyes.

It's not my physical eyes.

I see with my spiritual eyes within my heart.

I see my dreams; I see my talents.

I see my gifts and I receive it all.

No more fear.

No more running.

I've seen the goodness of your glory,

and I am embracing it all, even while my hands cover my eyes.

You have allowed me to see your spirit Lord.

Not with my physical eyes, but with my spiritual eyes.

You came and adjusted my eyes with your Holy Spirit,

 Even when I covered my eyes.

THEY TRIED TO BREAK ME, BUT GOD KEPT ME

Being young with no one to help me, who could I turn to?
I was mistreated, beaten, and mislead.
Who could I turn to?
I don't know what to do or which way to go.
Mind you, I'm just a child crying out loud.
GOD help me, please.
I belong to a family where they said they loved me in public.
In private, they are beating rings around my eyes.
The love is all a lie!
When dinner time came, I had to eat fast like a slave.
Grandma had me on a timer.
It was the hateful words that came out of her mouth,
that I will always remember.
She rushed me with those fire red gazing eyes.
They were so frightening.
She still couldn't break me even though she tried.
I cried at night so I couldn't be heard.
If grandma had heard me, she would have beat me.
There was one good thing I can honestly say I enjoyed.
She took me to church!
Little did she know that was the best thing she could have done.
A place to pray and call on GOD.
I would pray for her heart to change,
Because I refuse to let her break me.
I don't hate her or any of my family that played a part in my abuse, this I know.
As a child of GOD, His love and forgiveness pumps though my heart.
 I felt the presence of my Lord that day, I can't explain how.
GOD removed the pain.
I heard His voice say, "Hold on child. Don't give up or be dismayed."
"I will never leave you or forsake you. What I'm taking you through is a journey walk."

"So, hold on. Hold your head up high. I got you."

"The presence you feel is my Holy Spirit. Keep loving and forgiving those that hurt you."

"No matter what they try, you'll always stand strong with the help of GOD'S hands."

"I'm here to stay even when you cry, you must still pray."

I'm smiling inside.

I'm standing tall no matter what happen in my life!

Lord, you just made me strong like a cement wall.

They couldn't break me!

I SHOULD HAVE COME,
BUT I RAN WHEN GOD CALLED ME

You gave life to this beautiful creature that only you could have created.

You allowed this diamond, this beautiful jewel to be born.

In this world, that only you could have created, you blessed me with talents and gifts.

You anointed my lips with your precious Word.

You put love, forgiveness, and compassion in my heart.

A word to speak of your holiness,

To win souls and walk bold never folding when teaching.

Your word ministers to lost souls.

I know this for sure because you created me.

When I became lost,

When I turned a deaf ear and closed my eyes so that I could not see,

You still loved me.

Yes, you Lord; to you I belong.

You covered me in the blood of your son Jesus Christ.

It was me who said not yet to my Maker.

I did not answer the call my GOD.

I still had many things I wanted to do.

See, as I have gotten older, I realized the world will not satisfy me.

Yes, I was partying, drinking, fornicating, the whole nine yards!

See, I had to put you aside Lord because the lust of my eyes took over me.

I was excited about what the world had to offer me.

I'm not going to lie; I truly loved the ride of it all.

I know you said in your Word, John 3:16,

"GOD so loved the world that you gave your only son, Jesus."

Yes, that's what you said.

I do believe, but the world seems so lively and so free.

My mindset was I am grown, so I answer to no one!

Then it happened one day.

I got tricked up.

I wasn't receiving love from the world at all.

Not by my friends, no one!

The devil left me hanging all in a rut.

I was alone, no were to go, no one to talk to.

Man, my friends turned away and did not even know myself.

I'll just go to sleep right where I sit.

Here on the streets, I lost everything.

GOD, I need rest.

I was fast asleep when I heard a soft voice say to me...

It's not too late.

Take my hand and walk with me.

Let's talk; I've never left you.

I chase those I love.

My beautiful beloved creation, it's up to you to decide.

Free Will, good or bad allows you to choose this day He said.

I was awakened from my sleep by a lady that shook me.

She asked was I ok, and I told I her I was fine.

Something crossed my mind as I replied to her.

The stranger asked me my thoughts and I said to her,

Why didn't I come when GOD called me?

JUST LISTEN TO GOD'S CREATION

Just listen to GOD'S creations when the trees blow.

They really talking to each other saying Lord, Lord you are Holy.

When the river runs it cries out Glory, Glory.

When the rain falls upon my window, Oh joy!

When the mountains roar it cries out EMMANUAL, EMMANUAL wonderful Lord.

When the snow falls softly upon the cold ground,

There is truly warmth even under the surface of the earth.

You are pure and the righteous one.

There is no one like my Father.

Praise be to GOD.

Praise be the Creator of all.

Praises to His Son, Jesus Christ.

Jesus is the King of Kings and Lord of Lords.

He is the Prince of peace.

Praise be to the Father the greatest creation of all.

He is life everlasting.

He is the beginning and the end.

Holy, holy over and over again!

Amen.

Do you hear Him speaking in the mild, mild wind?

I hear him.

He is truly there.

HEAVEN'S SHOPPING CENTER, ONE NEAR YOU

Heaven's shopping center,

There is one near you.

This shopping center was quite different from other shopping centers I have ever seen.

Nothing as lovely as this one.

I went in one store.

Things were amazing.

Just the beauty of it blew my mind.

There was love hanging on the walls.

No charge.

I got that and put it in my heart.

Stepped in another store.

There was forgiveness sitting in a basket.

It was free!

I got that and put it in my heart as well.

I needed no bags.

I went in a third store, Oh GOD!

I was just going crazy.

I couldn't believe what I seen.

There was joy, peace, comfort, shouting, praying to the Lord.

There was glory to the Highest, but most of all,

There was witnessing and testifying.

My GOD!

Then there was the Word.

The holy Word.

Something better than silver and gold was the Holy Bible.

I needed no money or no credit card.

There was no charge.

Jesus paid it all.

24 hours a day.

Heaven's shopping center, one near you.

WHICH WAY DOES THE WIND BLOW?

Which way does the wind blow?
Which way does the wind blow?
I wonder which way does the wind blow.
I see GOD's trees blow to left and to the right.
Not in a crazy fearful way, but in a tender and sweet movement.
Then there is the soft blowing wind of GOD.
It keeps you in His loving hands.
GOD is so amazing when a wind of love blows.
A wind that is a wakeup call.
It comes blowing through my heart.
So, Lord, thank you for your strong and mighty wind.
It just truly blew in me.
Yes, Lord by your loving winds I am truly set free.

THIS WORLD IS NOT A FICTIONAL WORLD

This world is real.
It's not a fictional world.
People are lost living in a fictional state of mind.
Lost in the rules that they make up.
Trusting in the lies that the devil portray.
In your mind not believing that heaven and hell do exist.
Where you make your bed, you shall lay.
The devil telling them what they want to hear and however to live.
It's ok, you are untouchable he says.
You start to think the Lord will let you slide.
We truly know in our hearts that's a lie!
Heaven will be for the righteous.
Hell for the wicked.
This is not fiction.
This my friend is true.
Heaven or hell will await you.
It's the road that you chose.
This world is true.
I can tell you so because I was living a lie just as well.
The veil of sin on my face looking me right in the eyes.
I say YES to a different path today.
The Lord and GOD of my soul removed my veil.
Now I can see.
Longer am I waiting for my soul to go to hell.

SEVEN DAYS A WEEK

Seven days a week.
Monday was a slow day at work.
Tuesday, I started to work hard.
Wednesday I made plans.
Thursday, I am shopping for the party.
Friday, I picked up my friends for a night out.
Saturday was on and popping.
Sunday, I missed church, but the Lord understands.
Week two!
Monday I am just so tired.
Tuesday GOD was talking to me.
Wednesday GOD came in a vision to me.
Thursday, I hide in so much shame.
Friday, I tossed and turned.
I didn't finish out work this week.
Saturday, I cried out.
Please, Jesus save me because I am so tired.
Yes, a sinner I am.
Jesus forgive me, please.
Sunday, He gave me a church home to worship.
I went down in the water and He made me whole again.
Yes, I'm free from sin because GOD saved a wretch like me.

A COMPLAINING WORLD: WHY DO WE COMPLAIN?

We complain about things we pray so hard for.
We pray for a job but say it's too hard.
We pray for money but it's never enough.
We pray for a house but it's not nice or big enough.
We pray for love and we seem to never receive enough.
We pray for GOD's Holy Spirit to help us, but do we accept His help?
GOD gives us what we really need.
We as GOD'S people are never happy or pleased.
Stop thanking GOD only when things are going well.
Praise Him when our storms are not so good.
We get upset soon as a storm come our way.
Stop the complaining.
Learn to appreciate the smaller things,
So, when the greater things come you won't complain.
Learn to stay in your lane,
Pray, and wait on the Holy Spirit to steer you in the right direction.
GOD has chosen our paths a long time ago,
And we didn't even know it.

A MOTHER'S PRAYER FOR HER KIDS

A mother's prayer for her kids.
What lost souls they are.
I cried long years of tears.
If they only knew what they should fear.
They go on with their lives of gold.
They don't know how they have sold their souls.
But it's not too late to turn around.
GOD is waiting on them anyway.
Hell is not the way to go.
Darkness burning Lord Jesus.
I don't think they know.
If you change your minds and hearts to serve,
Get ready for the glory of GOD!
Trust and believe.
Lord, I know they won't leave.
Just trust and believe sons and daughters.
Your hearts and mind will be free.

KEEP YOUR HEAD UP AND SMILE AGAIN

Keep your head up.
Smile again.
Don't worry about a thing.
When trouble comes your way, stand still.
It's already worked out.
Keep your head up.
When folks don't care to understand, keep your head up.
Smile.
Just when you look around, there is the sound of GOD'S wonderful power.
My GOD.
Can't you see how He fixed it for you and me?
Strong winds may blow.
Smile.
Hold your head up high.
Stand in your storm and know that the Lord will hold you forever more.

Play 1
The Prayers Of A Praying Mother

This play is fictional. The characters names are Anna Brown, Joe Brown, and Pristina Brown. The family lives in Lake City, South Carolina. The family has been living in Lake City since Pristina was a baby. Joe is sixty-seven years old, and Anna is sixty years old. Pristina is twenty-one years of age. Joe owns a garage that his father left him. Anna works at the Lake City Hotel. Pristina is in her second year of college on a scholarship. The name of the college is Florence Darlington. Anna's co-worker's names are Karen Miller, Dawn Henry, and Ray-Ray Hopkins which is Pristina's boyfriend.

The prayer warriors are Anna's church friends: Sister Ruth, Sister Mae, Sister Susan, Sister Gwen, and Pastor Arnold Day. The Owner of the Lake City Hotel is Boss Lady. Pristina's best friend is Tasha Smith. She Works at the Lake City Get Money Bank.

This play is to encourage anyone that is going through some bad times, especially when it involves your kids or a family member. Don't give up. Trust GOD. You never know how He will turn it around. The Bible says to take all our burdens to the Lord, leave them there, and GOD will work them out. PSALM 55:22.

Act 1
Scene One
Joe and Anna's home

Narrator: Anna is up. It's Monday morning as usual. She's getting ready to prepare breakfast for Joe and herself.

Anna: Joe come on down here. Breakfast is ready. Every morning you move so slow.

Joe: Coming baby. Hold your bridges woman. You always in a hurry.

Narrator: Joe comes downstairs. Says good morning and they both sit down. Anna blesses the food. They both began to eat. Time has gone by, Anna and Joe are done eating. Joe hurries to prepare to get them to work. He doesn't want no trouble with the Boss Lady, Anna's boss. Anna and Joe both laughs and puts their coats on.

Joe: Dress warm baby, it's cold today. Thirty-two degree this morning.

Anna: Let's pray before we walk out that door baby.

Joe: Ok baby. Yes, we can't leave out without putting God first in all things, even this day.

Anna: Father God in the name of Jesus Christ, cover us as. You allow Joe and I to make it another day in Jesus's name, Amen.

ACT 1
Scene Two

Takes place in the car

Narrator: The prayer is over. Joe and Anna leave out the house. Joestarts up the carand their off to work. Joe pulls up at the Lake City Hotel where Anna works. Anna gets out the car and walks into the building. She punches her timecard in and begins to fill up her cart. She has thirteen rooms to clean. Anna gets on the elevator.

ACT 1
Scene Three

Takes place at Lake City Hotel

Narrator: She gets off on the fifth floor. Boss Lady is making her rounds on the floor as she does every morning. She is waiting to talk with Anna. Anna sees her boss and says good morning.

Boss Lady: Good morning Mrs. Anna. Look, I need you and the other ladies to stay the whole week to work late. Staff is short. The hours are from 8 am to 9 pm. Are you able to stay late?

Anna: Yes, not a problem. I'll stay to help out.

Narrator: Boss Lady leaves off that floor making her rounds on the other floors.

Anna: Lord, I'm tired. Give me the strength to carry on in Jesus's Christ name. (Pulling out her phone from her pocket calling her husband) Hey baby, Boss Lady asked if I could work late this week. Therefore, I need you to pick me up at 9 pm.

Joe: Yes, baby. I'll be there to pick you up then. See you later baby.

Anna: Ok baby, I'll see you later.

Narrator: Anna gets back to work. There are two knocks at the door. Anna opens the door and it is Dawn.

Dawn: Girl, look at you looking all tired. When are you going to let the young folks get a job? You know you need to retire.

Anna: I am ok. It's God that is keeping me honey. Don't you worry your pretty little head about me. Trust me, I'm fine.

Dawn: Yea, ok I hear you. Well, tell God to help you clean these thirteen rooms. (Laughing to herself)

Dawn: All jokes aside, if you need help, call me. Ok?

Narrator: Dawn leaves out the room, but there is another knock at Anna's door. Karen enters the room.

Karen: Hi, can I talk to you Mrs. Anna?

Anna: Yes, baby. This is starting to feel like a meeting in the upper room.

Karen: No, Mrs. Anna. I just wanted to let you know if you need me, I'm here for you. Ok? I know Dawn and I play a lot, but we are here if you need us. That's for real. You have our word.

Anna: (Smiling) Ok baby. I told Dawn if she wanted her job, she better get back to work.

ACT 1
Scene Four

Takes place in the car

Narrator: The day has gone by and Anna's shift is over. Joe picks up Anna from workand they are on their way home from a long day. Joe is driving really fast, and Anna tells him to slow down.

Anna: Slow down baby! I want to live not die. (They both start laughing)

ACT 1
Scene Five

Anna and Joe are in the car

Narrator: The week has flown by. Friday is here. No more late hours for the ladies at the Lake City Hotel. Joe picks up his wife from work. She gets in the car and they head home from the hotel. Anna and Joe pull up to the house.

ACT 1
Scene Six

Joe and Anna's living room

Narrator: Anna and Joe both enter the house. Anna sits in the living room. She's exhausted and her feet hurts really bad. Joe sees how tired she is and decides to make sandwiches for dinner.

Anna: Baby, thanks for the sandwich. It was good. Boss Lady worked us ladies this week like crazy. We really don't stand up for ourselves because Lord knows we need our jobs.

Narrator: The phone rings. Anna picks up after the second ring.

Anna: Hello, who's calling?

Pristina: Momma, it's me, Pristina.

Anna: Hi baby! I am so happy to hear from you. Everything ok?

Pristina: Yes momma. Everything is fine.

Joe: (Looks at Anna with a crazy look) Woman give me the phone. Let me talk to my baby.

Narrator: Anna gives Joe the phone.

Joe: Hi baby. I miss you so much. How is everything going on in school?

Pristina: Everything is fine daddy. I'll be home next Monday for two weeks. The dean decided to give us all a short break.

Joe: That sounds great. Do you need me to pick you up from the bus station?

Pristina: No, daddy. I'll get a cab. I'll be fine.

Joe: Here baby, you can talk to Pristina now.

Anna: Ok baby, we will talk with you later. Have a great day at school.

Narrator: Anna is so happy to hear the good news about their daughter coming home for a short break.

Anna: Baby, we have to do some cleaning, dusting, and maybe wipe down her windows in her bedroom.

Joe: Baby, look, I'll clean. I'm not wiping down any windows! (Starts laughing) Come on woman. Let's get ready for bed. We have to get up early to clean.

Act 2

Scene One

Brown family preparing for Pristina coming home for vacation

Joe and Anna's bedroom

Narrator: It's Saturday morning. Anna and Joe are up cleaning the house and it's coming together. Everything is looking good, and they are finally done. Anna says to Joe, "well let's get our clothes out for church tomorrow. We haven't been in the house of God in a month of Sundays." Joe and Anna started to head up for bed.

ACT 2
Scene Two

Narrator: Sunday morning and Anna and Joe are up out the bed. They began to get ready for church. Anna goes downstairs to prepare breakfast for the both of them while Joe is still getting dress.

Anna: Joe, Come on! Breakfast is ready. Lord that man is slow every morning. The same thing every morning. Joe, come on baby.

Joe: Woman, you going to stop calling me like that. I'm coming. I don't have on roller skates. Calm down Anna. That breakfast is not going to walk off the table baby.

Anna: Come on. Let's say grace and eat. Lord thank you for this hot meal in Jesus's name, Amen.

Joe: We better hurry up. Church starts at ten a.m. This breakfast was delicious. Well, I'm done. I see you are finished as well. Better get ready to head out baby.

Anna: Yea, let's get ready to go. Let me get our coats baby. I can't wait to see the look on those folks faces when we walk in the church doors. *(They both start laughing).*

CHURCH SERVICE

Takes place outside of the church

Narrator: Anna and Joe head out the house getting in the car. Joe starts it up and off they go to the church. It is three blocks down from where they live. Pastor Arnold is preaching from Roman 3:23, "For all have sinned and come short of the Glory of God." Everyone is enjoying the service. Church is over. Time had flown by. It is 2:45 in the afternoon and everyone are heading home.

Joe: Service was good. The word went forth. Yes, I truly enjoyed myself. Lord, all have Sinned. That's what the preacher said baby. All have sinned. I hope and pray in my heart we are living our best for the Lord.

Anna: Yes, Lord the word of God really blessed my heart. Yes, Lord my soul says yes Lord. So happy God is just so good, so good.

ACT 2
Scene Three

Joe and Anna's home

Narrator: Anna and Joe walks in the home. Anna is telling Joe that they will have sandwiches for dinner because she does not feel like cooking. Anna heads in the kitchento make the sandwiches. They both sit down to eat. Joe blesses the food, and they began to eat. They converse about the wonderful day they had. Some time had passed. They decided to head up for bed.

ACT 2
Scene Four

Narrator: It is now Monday morning and Anna is getting ready for the day. She is finally dressed, and breakfast is on the table. She begins to sing to herself. Pristina is on her way home and Joe is still getting dress.

Anna: (Laughing) I could not have said it better myself.

Joe: You done baby? Yes, I'm done. Let's get ready to go.

ACT 2
Scene Five

Takes place in car

Narrator: Joe and Anna have prayer before leaving the house and they are headed to work. Anna turns to Joe as he's driving. She thanks God because she does not have to work long hours this week.

Joe: Well baby, you are here. Don't work too hard or too slow. (Laughing) Have a great day baby.

Anna: (Laughing) You just be here at five o'clock. See you later.

Narrator: It's five o'clock. Joe has picked Anna from work.

Anna: Hello baby

Joe: Hello baby. How was work?

Anna: Everything was fine. I am just excited to see our daughter.

ACT 2
Scene Six

Joe and Anna's house

Narrator: They are both so excited because Pristina is paying them a visit. Pristina should be at the house waiting for them. Joe is driving as fast as he can to get home. Anna would say something about his driving fast, but her excitement did not allow her. They pulled up to the house and got out of the car. Anna can't wait to open the door. Pristina is sitting on the couch and greets them as they enter the house. She gives them both a big hug and lots of kisses.

Joe: I'm not working tomorrow because we are having a family day out. How about that? Yes, spending some quality time together is very important to me. Lady's, dinner, and a movie on me.

Anna: I'm calling out too. My boss hired three more people and Tuesdays are slow anyway.

Joe: Yes, our baby is home. Our baby is home. Thank you, Jesus.

Pristina: That sounds fine daddy going out will be fun.

Anna: Hello, Boss Lady. I'm calling out for Tuesday. I am having some family time with my daughter.

Boss Lady: Not a problem. I will see you Wednesday morning.

Anna: Yes, you will. Goodbye.

Pristina: I'm going to call Tasha. I told her I would be home today. She's going to stop by one day this week. We have a lot of catching up to do if that's ok with you guys.

Joe: Yes, that's fine. Not Tuesday. That's our day out together.

Anna: I haven't seen Tasha in a while. How is she doing?

Pristina: She's fine. Just working hard. She's at a bank. All that money is no joke.

Anna: Yes, your right baby. That is so true.

Narrator: Pristina calling Tasha.

Tasha: Hello. Hey girl. You home?

Pristina: Yes, I am home. Can't wait to see you, but it will have to be Thursday. We are going out Tuesday and I have something to do Wednesday.

Tasha: That's fine. See you then. Bye.

Narrator: Pristina, Anna, and Joe headed up for bed. It's been a long day. Everyone is Tired. Everyone says goodnight and goes to bed. Pristina is getting ready for bed. She heads to her bedroom. Her phone rings. She answers it and smiles. It's Ray-Ray on the other end.

Ray-Ray: Hey, baby. What's up? When can I come see you? You know I miss you girl.

Pristina: Ray-Ray stop playing baby. You know I have been leaving school to see you since school started. My mom and dad are taking me out to dinner and a movie tomorrow. You can come over Wednesday, ok?

Ray-Ray: Yea, that's cool. I guess I'll see you tomorrow. Bye baby. Talk to you Wednesday.

ACT 2
Scene Seven

Anna and Joe's house

Narrator: It's Tuesday morning. Everyone is up and getting ready for the day. Breakfast is ready and on the table. Everyone is now downstairs. Anna has blessed the food. They are eating and talking about the day. Pristina is excited about dinner and a movie. Time goes by and they are out enjoying the evening together. The dinner and movie is over, and they are returning home. They are ready to relax. They have entered the house and Pristina turn on the television. She begins to watch television. All of them together are talking amongst themselves.

Pristina: I am tired now. I'm going to bed. Goodnight mom and dad. You guy's should get some rest as well.

Joe: Yes, baby. She's right. We should turn in as well. Back to work tomorrow.

Anna: Ok, let's head on up. Good night Pristina. Sleep well baby.

Narrator: They all go into their rooms and off to sleep they go.

Act 3
Scene One
Takes place in the kitchen

Narrator: The night has gone by. It's now Wednesday morning. Anna is up preparing breakfast for everyone. She is so happy Pristina is home. She cooking a big breakfast singing and dancing around the kitchen. The food is done. Anna blesses the food, and they begin to eat.

Pristina: I'm done mama. May I be excused from the table?

Anna: Yes, baby. You may be excused. Well Joe, we better head out for work. I know it's going to be busy at my job.

ACT 3
Scene Two

Pristina's conversation with Ray-Ray

Pristina's bedroom

Narrator: Before leaving the house, Anna, Joe, and Pristina have prayer together. Both parents are on their way to work. Pristina is preparing for Ray-Ray to come over. She never told her parents about the company she was preparing to have. She has candles all around the bedroom and slow jams on to set the mood. She even has something sexy for her man. The doorbells ring. It's Ray-Ray.

Pristina: Hold up baby. I'm coming. (She opens the door) Hey baby.

Ray-Ray: Look at you girl! Looking all fine for your man. See, that's what I'm talking about. You getting all sweet for your baby.

Pristina: See, baby, I even have some candles burning too. I wanted to give a nice smell to the house. (Laughing to herself) Let's go upstairs so we can relax even better.

Ray-Ray: I feel you baby. I miss you girl. I'm ready to make you happy.

Pristina: Slow your roll baby. You're moving too fast. Look, we have time for all that stuff later. I need to talk to you Ray-Ray.

Ray-Ray: Talk about what? Look I didn't come here to talk. What's your problem? Stop playing and let's get down to business.

Pristina: Well, that's what got us in this mess now, getting down to business. Look man, stop playing around. I'm six months pregnant. I'm a big girl, but I'm not that big. My parents are going to know something is wrong sooner or later. I can't hide this forever. What are we going to do?

Ray-Ray: Girl, you are crazy. That's not my baby. I'm not claiming nothing. That's your problem.

Pristina: I'm not crazy! What do you mean? I'm crazy? Ray-Ray stop playing man. You know this is your baby. I have never been with no other man but you. Why are you doing this to me? *Pristina starts to cry.*

Ray-Ray: Well, technically, (Laughing out loud) you been lying to your parents for a long time and for real I believe you been lying to me as well.

Pristina: Man, I know I've been lying to my parents about not coming home when school breaks came around. That was only because you ask me to spend time with you and you also ask me to lie to my parents. Remember that? You said you love me Ray-Ray! When I told you I was pregnant the first time, you also said not to worry that everything would be alright. So, who's the liar now?

Ray-Ray: Girl, look. It's like this. When I was going to church that was all a front to get with you. That was a long time ago. We hooked up and I thought things were good. I knew you was a church girl, or was that a lie too? You knew in your heart your parents would not approve of us being together. I mean, come on. You knew I didn't know GOD then and I don't want to know GOD now. You fell for the lies I told you. Grow up and tell your parents you are pregnant, but please leave my name out of it. Matter of fact, this relationship is over between us. I'm claiming nothing. You're on your own, bye.

ACT 3
Scene three

Takes place in the kitchen

Narrator: Ray-Ray leaves the house and slams the door behind him. Pristina is sitting crying not knowing what to do. Joe and Anna are walking up to the door, just missing Ray-Ray by a couple of minutes. They call out to Pristina. She answers them both and goes downstairs to see what they wanted. Joe asks Pristina is everything ok. Pristina brushes her emotions off and tells him she is fine. Anna goes in the kitchen to start dinner.

Anna: You sure? You look like something is bothering you.

Pristina: Everything is fine. Why are you asking me? Everything is ok. Do you know something I don't know?

Anna: (Laughing) Well, if it's something we need to know, then let us in on it. We're just asking a question, that's all. It looks like something is on your mind. Well, anyway, I had the craziest dream last night. I was dreaming about fish in a small pond. The water was so crystal clear. You know my mother use to say when you dream about fish, someone is pregnant. Strange, you know. I wonder who it could be. Well, let me get dinner started. (Anna walks into the kitchen to start dinner).

Pristina: (Looks sad) Mom, I'm tired. I'm not eating this evening. I just want to rest.

Anna: Baby, you sure you're alright? I'm making your favorite tonight, roast beef Potatoes, and greens.

Pristina: No, not hungry. Going to bed. Love you momma.

Anna: Ok baby. Go on and get some rest. I pray you feel better.

Joe: (Comes in the kitchen) Baby, there's something going on with that child and I'm going to find out what it is. One minute she's happy and the next, it's like she done saw a ghost. Something just not right.

Anna: Yes, I felt it in my spirit that something is wrong. Maybe she will talk about it with us tomorrow if she chooses. I'm praying for her. I don't like to see my baby upset.

Joe: Yes, we just have to pray and trust GOD. We do know that He can work it out. Well, is dinner ready? I'm ready to eat! I'm hungry.

ACT 3
Scene Four

Takes place in Pristina' bedroom

Narrator: Anna and Joe begin to eat, talking amongst themselves. Pristina is still in her room feeling sad. Joe and Anna are finished dinner. Anna goes and check on Pristina before she gets ready for bed. Anna says goodnight to Pristina then off to bed they all go.

Pristina: (She is still upset. She gets down on her knees and starts to pray to GOD) God, please help me. What did I do LORD? I have gotten myself in a lot of mess and I don't know what to do. I have been living a lie. I have turned my back on you for lust and a man. Help me, Father. I don't know what to do. Help me, please. I need you. I don't know which way to turn.

Narrator: Pristina gets up and sits on the side of her bed. She picks up the Bible fromthe night table. She hasn't read it in some years. She begins to open it up and she remembers proverb 3:5 "Trust in the Lord with all your heart and lean not to your own understanding." She stops crying and talks to GOD even more. "LORD, please send your Holy Spirit to give me the help I need. She starts to feel the presence of GOD and she feels safe in GOD'S arms again. She thanks God for love and closes out her prayer with amen.

Pristina: GOD, I really thought you were angry with me because I've truly made a mess of things. I am so sorry. Please forgive me.

Narrator: Pristina felt a strong presence in her room. She heard a loud voice say t Her. The voice said, "Child, GOD don't want you to look back at your mess. It will distract you from what's in front of you. See, the devil wants to remind you of your past and mistakes. He brings up your failures and will even tell you we messed up GOD'S plans. You are where the Father wants you. Don't worry. Move forward." The voice is gone and Pristina falls asleep.

ACT 3
Scene Five

Narrator: It's the next day. Anna is making breakfast and the doorbell rings. It's Tasha for Pristina. Anna opens the door to let Tasha in and allows her to have a seat. Anna calls for Pristina. Pristina pops her head out of her room and asks for Tasha to come upstairs. Tasha walks in Pristina's room and they began to talk.

Tasha: Hey, what's up? Look, we need to talk. Did you tell your parents about your Situation yet?

Pristina: No, I don't need you running your mouth. I have everything under control! Let's talk about something else. We haven't seen each other or talked in while, so I'm sure you have something else to talk about.

Tasha: Ok, you have to talk to your parents sooner or later. I think today would be a great time to do it.

Pristina: I know. Please change the subject. Talk about something else.

Tasha: Well, work is great. I have my own house and a new car. GOD is truly good to me. Yes, before you even ask, I'm still serving the Lord. You know there's nothing wrong with that at all.

Pristina: That's nice girl. Look, I am not putting you out, but I really need to rest. Being six months pregnant is a lot of work. *Pristina laughs to herself*

Tasha: I understand. Well, let me go. I'll call you sometime this weekend if I get a chance. Bye, be bless Pristina and GOD still loves you.

Pristina: I know. Bye. Talk with you later.

ACT 3
Scene Six

Takes place in the kitchen

Narrator: It's now Friday morning. Anna has prepared a big breakfast for the Family. It's time for their daughter to return back to college and this time her father will be driving her back to school.

Anna: Joe, come on and tell Pristina to come down as well. Breakfast is ready.

Narrator: Joe and Pristina are down for breakfast, but Pristina says she's not Hungry. Anna is not understanding why her daughter is not eating.

Anna: Is everything alright baby?

Pristina: Yes ma'am. Everything is fine. (She drops her head).

Joe: (Starts eating and talking to Anna in a low voice as they look at their daughter with a look that's not pleasing).

Pristina: Mom, dad. Is everything ok?

Joe: Baby girl, is there something you need to tell me and your mother?

Pristina: No daddy, why?

Anna: Baby, are you sure? You know you can talk to us about anything.

Pristina: What is wrong with you guys? You both act like I'm hiding something from you.

Joe: Wait a minute baby girl. Did you think for one minute you were fooling me? I don't know about your mother, but I knew something was wrong when you started turning down food. You done brought shame to our family and you need to start talking! We are waiting right now.

Anna: Joe, please let her talk. Let her talk, Joe. Please don't do this. She will talk when she is ready.

Joe: No, Anna I went through her bags. I don't know why, but I did. I found the letter she can't go back to school. They kicked her out! She's been sneaking off seeing that Ray-Ray boy we told her to stay away from him Anna.

Pristina: Daddy, I'm sorry for embarrassing and shaming the family. Sorry for lying about school. I don't know what happen and where it all went wrong, but it did. Daddy I'm so sorry.

Anna: Pristina, we always talked and prayed about everything. We serve GOD because He's a good GOD all by himself. Yes, Lord! Don't you know nothing we do is new under the sun? Nothing! "ECCLESIASTES 1:9" the word of GOD is real, and it don't come back void.

Pristina: Momma, daddy, I'm sorry. I told Ray-Ray and he just pushed me away. He called me a liar and said he wants nothing to do with me or the baby. What I'm going to do?

Joe: I'll tell you both what I'm going to do! I'm going to kill him dead. That's what I'm going to do. This is my little girl. It's not going down like that. He will pay for this. Don't you worry, I got this.

Anna: Joe, don't you ever talk like that. You know GOD will make your enemies your footstool. Read it, Joe! PSALM 110:1 and PSALM 46:10, "Be still and know that I'm God. I will be exalted among the nations, I will be exalted in the earth." God will fix it. We have to turn it over to Him, Joe. We have to trust Him with all our heart. Faith as little as a mustard seed. Yes, Lord.

Pristina: Daddy, I'm sorry. I prayed and asked God to help me not to do wrong. The Holy Spirit spoke to me daddy. He told me to look forward and don't look back at my past. So that's what I am going to do. I am trusting GOD. I don't know how things will work out, but I'm believing He will work it out, daddy.

Joe: Baby girl, I just wanted the best for you, and I still do. I'm your father and fathers are supposed to make sure their children are safe and not lacking for anything. Do you understand what I'm trying to say to you baby girl? I just want the best for my daughter.

Pristina: DADDY, you have done more than enough for me and I'm grateful for everything.

Narrator: Pristina gives her dad and mom a hug and tells them both how muchshe loves them. They too hug her with a tight hug.

Anna: We are a family that loves and serves the LORD, our GOD. In this house we shall serve the LORD. This baby will be a blessing to this house no matter if it's a boy or a girl. A blessing is truly on the way. You both know I'm a praying mother. I have always prayed for my family day and night. When you both don't even know, I'm on my knees or in my closet. We are going to pray for Ray-Ray. We will pray that GOD changes his heart one day and that he will ask, what must he do to be saved! Yes, Lord! Any man can change if they want to be changed.

Act 4
Scene One
The family invite for Ray-Ray

Joe: Maybe if we have him over for dinner, we can talk with him and see for ourselves how he really feels.

Anna: Yes, that sounds great. Pristina will you give him a call?

Pristina: Yes, I'll call him. (Calls Ray-Ray) It's all set up for Saturday evening.

Narrator: Anna is up making breakfast for herself, Joe, and Pristina. They have a long day ahead of them and Anna decided to invite four of her prayer warriors to the house. They are also coming for dinner. What Pristina don't know is that these four women are going to be praying for Ray-Ray. Pristina and Joe are eating breakfast and talking amongst themselves. Anna is singing to herself "o happy days." She repeats the song over and over while she's washing dishes. Pristina and Joe are done eating. The day has finally gone by.

Pristina: Mama, you sure do have it looking like we about to have church up in here.

Anna: Baby, yes, we are. When us prayer warriors come together, that's what happens.

Pristina: Mama, I thought we were just going to talk to Ray-Ray after dinner?

Anna: Oh, we are going to talk and pray. We might just even sing. All depends on the Holy Spirit baby.

Pristina: Oh, ok this is going to be something! My Lord, help me. I need to sit down. This is crazy.

ACT 4
Scene Two

Prayer warriors arrive

Narrator: The prayer warriors ring the doorbell. Pristina opens the door. Sister Ruth, Sister Susan, Sister Gwen, and Sister Mae enter. The women greet Pristina. Sister Mae in a sarcastic tone tells Pristina she heard she was having a baby and not to have anymore. Sister Mae goes on to ask Pristina if she knew what it took to be a mother. Pristina just walked away.

Sister Gwen: Sister Mae, you have no right saying that stuff to that child. What is wrong with you?

Sister Susan: That's right! We are not here to judge her. We are here to pray and trust that GOD will work everything out for this family. So, stop playing GOD because you are far from being Him.

Sister Ruth: That is right ladies. Remember Romans 3:10 "THERE IS NO ONE RIGHTEOUS, NOT ONE" That includes us! Let us not throw stones.

Narrator: Sister Ruth rolls her eyes and goes into the dining room where they would eat. Anna came out of the kitchen and says, "Praise the Lord ladies! Glad you all made it." Joe comes downstairs. He is wondering why the prayer warriors are in the dining room because Anna did not tell him they were coming over. Joe turns to his daughter. Well, your mother done did it again baby girl! Joe keeps on laughing very loudly. Pristina is getting nervous, not knowing what was about to go down. Someone is at the door. Pristina opens the door and it's Ray-Ray.

Ray-Ray: What's up?

Pristina: Hey.

Anna: Let's all get ready to sit and eat this great dinner. Yes Lord!

Joe: Father GOD, bless this food and everyone around this table in JESUS'S CHRIST Name, Amen. Ok, good food. Let's eat. I'm hungry.

Anna: Well, Ray-Ray I'm going to get right to the point. We asked you to come because Joe and I needed to know why you pushed our daughter away like she's trash? I'm not fussing, just asking a question?

Ray-Ray: First of all, you ask me here to question me about your daughter? I thought this was just a friendly dinner. I don't owe anyone any answer about me, or what happen between me and your daughter. You all don't know me. Yes, you watched me grow up in church, but a lot has changed since then. When my father left me and my mother, she died from cancer. See, GOD took my mom from me and my father was a drunk. He never cared about my mother or me. So, you want to know something about me? Well, I'm a drug dealer, just ask your daughter. She knew what I was even when I was going to church.

Anna: Son, I didn't know this. I thought your family just gave up on GOD and left the
church. You all just stop coming.

Ray-Ray: No, if you had asked, you would have known. You never asked! See, you and your husband already judged me from the beginning. No, I don't believe in GOD and GOD don't love me. He didn't love my father or my mother either. He allowed all this drama to come upon our family. I'll never serve GOD, never! I hate my life. I wouldn't be this way if my mom was still alive. I'm no good. I'm nothing! Yes, that's my baby, so just stay off my back.

Narrator: Ray-Ray drops his head and began to cry because truly he's hurting inside. Joe and Anna begin to pray and cry out to GOD for the young man. They wanted him to see that GOD haven't forgotten him and that GOD loves him too. Sister Ruth, Sister Susan, Sister Gwen, and Sister Mae got down on their knees and began to pray. They were calling out to GOD on Ray-Ray's behalf. Ray-Ray falls to his knees as well along with the prayer warriors. Sister Ruth begins to sing, "I need thee o Lord, I need thee," and the spirit of the Lord fell upon everyone in the room. It was truly the mighty power of GOD moving. When Sister Ruth finish singing, everyone got up off their knees. They turned to Ray-Ray and embraced him with love.

Ray-Ray: I have decided to give my life to JESUS CHRIST. I'm coming back to church, and Pristina, I want to apologize for hurting you. I'm going to get a job and be the best father I can be for our child. (He gives her a hug and she hug him back).

Anna: THANK YOU FATHER, GOD. We never count nobody out. GOD hasn't counted you or me out, so why should we? No one has the power to save anyone. GOD does the saving, we win the souls for Him. We don't have a hell or heaven to put no man.
Joe: Amen, GOD has the first and last word, right baby? (Joe smiling).

Anna: Yes, baby. Pristina, I spoke with the Dean. You can go back to school and finish your last three months and graduate. I know the power of prayer because I'm a praying mother that prays for my family. Mothers all over the world needs to pray without ceasing. We all should pray, but when a mother prays, there is a different level of desperation. Amen.

Narrator: Everyone was so happy for Ray-Ray and Pristina. Prayer truly works! Whatever it is that you might go through, remember GOD is truly able to do just what He said He would do.

Play 2
The Marriage Retreat

This is a fictional play. The character names are Howard Smalls, Danielle Smalls, Paul Smalls, and Jason Smalls. The play is based out of the city of Philadelphia, Pennsylvania and Minneapolis, Minnesota. The play will open up in Philadelphia on Horton street. This play is based on a family that is not saved or have not accepted salvation from the Lord. They are having problems in their marriage. Two of their friends give them some advice on where to get help to save their marriage. The friends encourage them both to join a marriage retreat for counseling. The friend's names are Marry Brown and Kevin Brown. The two people that founded the retreat are Joe Thomas and Constance Thomas. Howard and Danielle will be leaving for the airport on January 3,2017, Monday morning. They will be in Minnesota for a week and then return home, prayerfully. They both return home changed people.

Act 1
Scene One

Starts off with morning routine. It's a cold morning in the city of Philadelphia. It's 29 degrees outside. Its Monday morning and the Smalls family is getting ready to start their day.

Danielle: Good morning, honey.

Howard: Good morning, baby.

Danielle: Boys, get ready for school.

Boys: Ok, mom.

Howard: I really don't feel like going to work today.

Danielle: Why? You know we need the money. These bills are killing us.

Howard: Is that all you think about?

Danielle: No, it's not, but you always wake up with the same attitude and I'm tired of hearing it.

Howard: Well, that's too bad. You know you sure do have a lot to say this morning and I'm not trying to hear it.

Danielle: (Gives Howard a look, rolls her eyes, and walks out the bedroom).

Danielle: Boys, get ready for school, please? Come downstairs on time for breakfast.

Boys: Ok, mom. Coming down now.

Howard: I have to do a double tonight, so don't wait for me.

Danielle: You always have to do a double, but your paycheck never shows that you worked doubles. You have also been coming home smelling like perfume, explain that.

Howard: I told you before, I'm working. If you don't believe me, that's on you.

Dannielle: (Looks at Howard, shakes her head, gets the boys, and leaves out the house).

Boys: Bye, dad.

Howard: Bye, boys. Have a great day at school. Can't say that for everybody.

Boys: (Talking in the back of the car while mom is driving them to school).

Paul: I'm sick and tired of mom and dad fussing all the time.

Jason: Yes, all they do is fuss, fuss, fuss. They are just never happy anymore.

Danielle: (Looks through her rear mirror at the boys, drops her head in sorrow, and continues to drive).

Danielle: (Pulls up in front of the school) Ok you guys. We are here. Have a great day, love you. (The boys get out) Have a great day as well mom. (They both walkinto the school building).

Act 1
Scene Two

Narrator: Meanwhile, Howard is at the job and he's not feeling so happy about thismorning's conversation with his wife. He decides to tell his friend Tommy about their emotional problems.

Tommy: Man, are you going to be ok? You both need to learn how to talk and listen to one another, that's all.

Howard: My wife always thinking that I have somebody else because I work late. Man, if she keeps this up, it just might happen! You feel me?

Tommy: Man, you know darn well you not going to cheat on your wife. Learn how to talk with one another.

Tommy: Stop fussing. Neither one of you are ever going to hear anything because you both seem like your blaming each other for things that's probably not that deep.

Howard: Man, I'm going to work. Talk with you later.

Narrator: Howard starts to work, and Tommy shakes his head then walks away.

Act 1
Scene Three

Narrator: Meanwhile, Danielle does homecare for a close friend that she has been friends with for over six years. Danielle cooks, cleans, and care for Marry Brown and Kevin Brown. Marry is watching Danielle's attitude. Marry thinks Danielle is mad about being at work.

Marry: Is everything alright? You don't seem like yourself today.

Danielle: Yes, girl, I'm fine. Just emotional problems in the marriage, that's all.

Marry: Do you want to talk about it?

Danielle: No, I'm fine. I came to work. Just let me do my job. I'm good.

Marry: (In a sarcastic tone) Ok, you got it. Get to it sister. (Laughs to herself).

Danielle: I'm fine!

Narrator: Danielle is done all of her work for the day and she waves to the Browns as she walks out the door.

Marry: Ok, bye.

Danielle: Bye.

Act 1
Scene Four

Narrator: Danielle and the boys are on their way home from a long day of work and school. Danielle and the boys enter the house.

Danielle: Boys, get your homework done. I'm going to get dinner started.

Boys: Ok, mom.

Danielle: Boys come and set the table. Dinner is ready.

Boys: Ok, mom.

Danielle: You guys done your homework?

Boys: Yes, mom.

Paul: We are done.

Narrator: Danielle and the boys are sitting at the table eating dinner. The boys are talking amongst themselves in a low voice. Sharing about their day and the things that occurred in school. Time has flown. They are done eating.

Danielle: Ok, boys. Help me clean the table.

Boys: Ok.

Narrator: Danielle and the boys are off to watch some television. Meanwhile, dad is
still at work.

Danielle: Paul and Jason the television goes off at nine-thirty. There is school tomorrow you guys.

Jason: Can we please stay up mom, please?

Danielle: No, Jason. You don't like to get up in the morning. Nine-thirty the television is off. That's final!

Narrator: They all go into their bedrooms to watch television.

Act 2
Scene One

Narrator: It's nine-thirty. Danielle and the boys are in bed and off to sleep. It's now the next day, Tuesday morning. Danielle is getting up to prepare breakfast for her and the boys. Before going downstairs to the kitchen, she wakes up the boys. Paul and Jason get up to get ready for school and eat breakfast.

Boys: Ok. We are up.

Narrator: The boys are up, dressed, and heading downstairs for breakfast.

Paul: Good morning, mom.

Danielle: Jason, you not going to say good morning?

Jason: Good morning and why do I have to go to school???

Danielle: Boy, you better eat and get yourself ready to leave.

Narrator: (Danielle laughs sarcastically) Everyone is eating, and dad is still at work. Danielle and the boys are talking amongst themselves.

Paul: We are done mom.

Danielle: Ok, you guys. Let us go. (They leave out the house to start their day).

Narrator: Danielle is not talking much this morning.

Paul: Mom, are you ok?

Danielle: Yes, I'm fine. I'm just tired. Ok boys, we are here. Love you both and see you later.

Boys: Ok mom. See you later.

Narrator: Cell phone ringing. It' Howard calling.

Danielle: Hello.

Howard: Hello. I'm on my way home.

Danielle: Ok, see you later.

Act 2
Scene Two

Narrator: Danielle is just getting to work and signing her time sheet.

Marry: Hello girl. How is everything going?

Danielle: Ok, I guess. Just a little tired, that's all.

Marry: Look, anytime you guys want to talk, we are here for you both.

Danielle: Ok (Starts to work).

Kevin: Look. Girl you and Howard need to just talk. We would love to talk with you both. We love you guys.

Danielle: Yea, I hear you both. Maybe one day, who knows.

Act 2
Scene Three

Narrator: Meanwhile, Howard just got in from work. He is hungry and looking in the refrigerator for something to eat. He's fussing because there's not a plate for him from last night or breakfast from this morning.

Howard: I don't believe this. She didn't put up a plate for me, like I don't live here. ok. It's cool. I'm going to get some sleep. I'm too tired to cook anything. This is so unreal.

Act 3
Scene One
Confrontation At The Dinner Table

Narrator: The day is over, and Danielle is off work. She picks up the boys from school. They are on their way home. Danielle and the boys pull up to the house and enter.

Howard: (Hears the door open and comes downstairs still upset).

Danielle: Hey baby.

Howard: Hey baby, so what I don't live here anymore? I mean I work and help out around this house, so am I missing something? I can't get a plate of food when I come home? Tell me something, please.

Danielle: Why do you always start? There is plenty to eat. Learn how to cook because I contribute as well to this house. Thank you very much!

Howard: Let me tell you something, when I met you, you had nothing. How you acting funny all of a sudden? Please, get a grip on yourself woman.

Danielle: You know what! If you are not happy about the way things are going on around here, then maybe you should just leave. We don't need you, if you don't want to be here. You find every reason to start an argument! Not today!

Narrator: Meanwhile, the boys are listening, and they are upset.

Paul: (Starts yelling) Stop please! What is wrong with you guys? I hate it here! I wish I was in another family!

Jason: Me too! (Starts to cry).

Howard: (Grabs his coat).

Danielle: Where are you going?

Howard: None of your business! (Slams the door).

Danielle: (Goes into the kitchen and starts dinner). Paul and Jason, come here. I want to talk with the both of you. (The boys sit down) I'm sorry about all of this. It has not been great between me and your dad for very long time. Maybe one day it will get better, but you two do not need to worry about us. Married people go through things. Remember there will be good days and bad days in life. Dinner will be ready soon.

Boys: (Just listening and walks away after Danielle is finished).

Narrator: Phone rings two times. Danielle picks up the phone to answer. It's Marry.

Danielle: Hello, hello! (With a loud voice, crying).

Marry: What's wrong? Is everything ok?

Danielle: No, I don't know how much more I can take from Howard. I'm so sick and tired of this.

Marry: What's wrong? What is going on?

Danielle: I don't think we are in love with each other anymore. All we do is fuss. I thought I was going to rip out his eyes today. He made me so angry! He was fussing and yelling around our kids. This is just crazy. It's not making any sense at all.

Marry: Look girl, me and my husband would really love to talk with you guys, please. I'm saying, just come listen to our story. We would like to share some information with you both.

Danielle: I don't know if he will even listen to me. We both said some hateful things to each other.

Marry: Just let things die down, and talk to him in the morning before you both leave for work.

Danielle: Ok girl. Look, I have to feed the boys. I'll talk with you tomorrow. Love you, bye.

Marry: Ok bye. Love you too.

Narrator: Danielle is done cooking for the boys. The boys come downstairs, and they all sit together. They begin to eat. It's very quiet. Dinner is now over. Everyone gets up from the table and cleans the kitchen. Danielle puts a plate up for Howard and they all head upstairs. Howard comes in and sees his food sitting on the table. He warms it up in the microwave, takes it out, and begins to eat. He eats fast because he is tired from work. He's done and off to bed he goes. He gets to the bedroom not saying anything to his wife. He leaves out of bedroom and goes to check on the boys. He kisses them both on the head and goes back into his bedroom still not talking to his wife. He gets in bed and goes to sleep.

Danielle: (Taps Howard on the shoulder) Are you sleep?

Howard: I was.

Danielle: Did you get your plate?

Howard: Yes, thank you.

Danielle: You are welcome. What do you think about having dinner with the Brown's on Saturday?

Howard: Why?

Danielle: Just something different

Howard: Ok, I guess.

Danielle: Ok, then I will let them know it's a go. Goodnight.

Howard: Goodnight.

Act 4
Scene One
Dinner With The Brown Family

Narrator: Danielle and Howard are getting ready for Saturday's dinner at the Browns. It's Friday. The boys are going to their aunt's house to stay overnight. Danielle and Howard drops the boys off. Danielle and Howard return home and the both of them are tired and decided to take a nap. The night has gone by and it is now Saturday morning. They are preparing for this evening's dinner out. It is time for them to leave the house. They have arrived at the Brown's house. Marry and her husband is sitting in the living room when the doorbell rings two times.

Marry: Who is it??

Danielle: Open the door its cold out here!

Narrator: Marry opens the door and Danielle and Howard walks in the house. They both say hello to the Browns. They say hello back to the both of them. Marry and Kevin began to share with Danielle and Howard about their marriage. They told them of how they too had a lot of problems and felt like there wasn't any hope for them as well. They also were on the verge of giving up on everything they built together, but one day they decided to go to church. They did not know that the pastor would speak their whole life not even knowing them. It may sound crazy, but we decided that day to go up to the front of the church for prayer. We wanted our marriage to work. We even went a step further, we accepted salvation. We wanted to be saved and seen a change afterwards. We both realized that we needed GOD. That's the glue that holds us together. Jesus Christ is our foundation that gives us the peace we needed, the love, and forgiveness for one another. It was GOD all along and if you guys are ready for that peace, you can have it too. You both have to decide when you're ready to give it over to GOD. Marry surprised them with two round trip tickets for the marriage retreat in Minnesota for one weeks. This was so Daniella and Howard could get the help they needed. Marry was certain that this would save their marriage. Danielle took the tickets and thanked them both. They said their goodbyes and went home.

Act 4
Scene Two

Danielle and Howard's house

Danielle: We better get packed. Our plane leaves Monday morning at twelve a.m. Thank GOD the boys will be able to stay with their aunt.

Howard: Yes, that was nice of her.

Danielle: Yes, we better turn in for bed. Everything is packed and ready to go. Goodnight.

Howard: Yea, goodnight.

Act 4
Scene Three

Leaving for the marriage retreat.

Narrator: Danielle and Howard have left for the airport. They left a little early to be on time. They have entered the airport and aboard their flight. They get their tickets punched by the airline attendant and take their seats. They are now off to Minnesota for the marriage retreat.

Danielle: Are you alright?

Howard: I don't know. I really don't want strangers in our business. I know you don't care, but I do.

Danielle: Why do always think the worst of me? Like, I don't know anything.

Howard: What?

Danielle: I'm not going to say another word, it's all good.

Narrator: Danielle closes her eyes and goes to sleep.

Howard: Yea, I'm going to do the same. That's the best thing we are doing right so far.

Act 4
Scene Four

Narrator: They both arrive at the airport to Minnesota and a cab is waiting for the both of them. The cab is holding up a sign with their names on it. They get in the cab and off they go. The driver lets them know it's just ten minutes away. Both of them seem nervous, not saying a thing. The driver arrives at the retreat and tells them to enjoy their stay. They grab their luggage and enter the lobby. It's around ten in the morning, and the Smalls are very tired from the flight.

Act 4
Scene Five

Constance: (Greets the both of them in the lobby).

Joe: Welcome to the marriage retreat. We know your names. We received your paperwork from your friends back home, so we will show you to your room and let you get comfortable. We will get started with our day shortly, ok?

Howard: Look, I don't like all that hugging and touching.

Danielle: Please, what is wrong? You know we need to make this marriage work. If not, baby then say your goodbye now.

Howard: Whatever! Don't push me woman.

Danielle: Man, let us go down for breakfast. I don't have time for this. It's too early in the morning.

Narrator: Danielle and Howard go down for breakfast. They have breakfast together with the other couples that's there as well. Time has gone by and they are done eating. Constance and Joe are showing them around the pool area and the game room. They also showed them the prayer rooms just in case they needed time to talk with GOD. Constance shared that there would be a meeting with every couple that showed up so, they could get to know one another. The meeting starts at seven-thirty this evening. There are four other couples that's there as well. It is now time for the meeting. Everyone is entering the room and it's time to get things started.

Act 5
Scene One

Narrator: Everyone say hello and takes a seat.

Howard: I'm going to be honest; I really don't want to be here. Our marriage is fine. Thank you.

Danielle: No, it's not. It's a hot mess. You need to grow up and be the man I first met.

Howard: Look, you're telling everyone about our life. I don't know these people and I'm not going to participate in this silly nonsense. You talk. I'm good.

Narrator: Danielle drops her head and says nothing.

Joe: Look, Howard. No, you don't have to be here, but someone cared enough to get you both tickets to save your marriage. No, you don't have to be here, sir. You don't even have to share your story, but all of you that is here are going through something or else you wouldn't be here. My wife and I would love to help you all if we can, and if you allow us. It's really up to everyone in this room. Everyone has decided to share their story.

Narrator: Howard still not feeling it. He says nothing and Danielle has not opened upeither.

Danielle: Well, it's like this; when we first met things were amazing. We did so many wonderful things together. He would come through for me all the time. I didn't need for anything, then once the babies came years later, the drama started. I mean, it's like a living hell! Something has to give, or we can just go our separate ways. Yes, I would love to work things out, but if my husband doesn't want to, then it's just a waste of time being here. That's all I have to say for now.

Constance: How is your sex life? Do you fight physically and say nasty things to each other? Mental abuse is the worst thing. Do you guys know the Lord, Jesus Christ, as your personal savior?

Danielle: No, we don't hit each other, and our sex life is poor. It doesn't happen actually. Yes, we do say nasty things to each other. No, we do not know the Lord. We never go to church because we just don't have the time.

Constance: See John 3:16 "for God so loved the world that he gave his only Son to die on the cross for our sins, so we would have everlasting life." Hallelujah!!!! I get so excited when I talk about my Lord.

Danielle: Well, we don't know anything about the Bible. Like I was saying, we don't go to any church, just don't have the time.

Joe: Howard and Danielle, without GOD in your lives, the devil has legal access to anything he wants concerning you to. The foundation of JESUS CHRIST is a must because the devil will have a field day with your minds that will one day destroy your lives.

Howard: Here we go again talking about the Bible. What does that have to do with our marriage and my wife nasty attitude? I really don't want to hear this at all.

Joe: Look, Howard. The word of GOD has a lot to do with it. Without GOD, you're just making your bed in hell. You both have two beautiful boys together. Just think, what would happen to them if you two divorced? You both need to raise them up the way GOD intended for them to go, not the ways of the world. Isaiah 55: 8-9.

Constance: Yes, Amen! So true. Well, it's nine p.m. We will return back here tomorrow, same time. We just want Howard and Danielle to join us then because of the short week they will have with us. The other couples, you guys have a two week stay. We will get with you in the earlier sessions. Goodnight everyone.

Narrator: Everyone says good night and they all exit out the room. Everything is quiet and Danielle and Howard are resting up for tomorrow.

Act 5
Scene Two

Narrator: Time has gone by and it is now Tuesday morning. Everyone is meeting for breakfast, and then a little shopping at twelve p.m. to get to know one another. Meanwhile, Constance and Joe are setting up for the seven-thirty meeting with Howard and his wife. The day has departed and it's time to meet up with one another. There are two knocks at the door.

Constance: Come in.

Howard: Good evening

Danielle: Good evening

Narrator: They both take a seat. Constance opens up with prayer to set the atmosphere in the room. Joe holds her hand and joins the prayer. Howard and his wife are very quiet, feeling uncomfortable. Constance is done praying.

Joe: Howard, what would you like to talk about? You were so unsure the first time we spoke at the first meeting. Open up, it's just us. Whatever is said in this room stays in this room.

Howard: Well, for one, I don't know you people. So, for me to open up, it's not that easy. I don't know where to start.

Constance: Just speak from your heart.

Howard: When we first got married and had our two boys, everything was great, at least I thought. My wife didn't complain about anything because I always did what a man should do, but later down the line, all she does is complain. She accuses me of cheating and say I don't do enough in her eyes. I'm tired of it! The way I feel, if things don't get better, we can file for a divorce. Since we are here, I guess I will see how this goes.

Joe: Son, everything wasn't all that great with me and my wife either. We had some great times and some really bad times. It's all a part of your growth. We also played the blame game and the happiness started to grow dark. Someone shared their story with us, and a friend sent us to a marriage retreat. You're not going to believe this, but this is the same one we went to. We wanted to impact lives by helping others. The people that owned this retreat passed away and left this place for my wife and I. GOD saw the good in our hearts to help others, and that's what we are going to do. Just let us in.

Howard: I hear you.

Constance: Danielle you can start if you like.

Danielle: I feel like a maid and not his wife. 'Baby, do this, do that.' We don't do anything together anymore. He told me the sky is the limit. What a lie that was! 'I'll never need for nothing,' he said and that was a lie! It's like he stopped caring, and I'm sick of it. He does nothing for the boys anymore, always brushing it off saying they fine. I'm here to try, that's all I can do, is try. That's all I have to say.

Narrator: Everyone gets quiet.

Constance: See, the problem is that you talk and don't listen. You both want to be right about everything. Believe it or not, it's not going to work out. Things are not going to always go your way, for neither of you. You both must grow up and learn to talk to one another. One at time, and then listen to what the other person has to say. You're not going to agree all the time, and that's fine. You both need Christ in your lives. That's the only way things are going to change, trust me. Learn to forgive one another. Stop going to bed mad and waking up mad over something that's really nothing.

Narrator: The time has been far spent. They are closing the meeting out.

Constance: (Turns to the both of them) I would love for you two to take Wednesday and Thursday to talk and listen to one another. Friday, we would like to talk with the both of you alone, is that ok?

Act 5
Scene Three

Narrator: Wednesday and Thursday quickly arrived. Howard and Danielle decided to take time out to talk and listen to each other. They both cried together, prayed a little, and even laughed a little. They started to really just embrace each other. They were so excited. They couldn't wait for Friday morning to attend the meeting. It's now Friday morning. Howard and Danielle are up and getting ready for breakfast. They decided to eat in the room until it was time for the meeting. It's time for the meeting, so they enter the room. The four of them greet each other and the talking begins. Danielle goes first.

Danielle: Well, I thought about everything the both of you said to me and my husband. We talked and we listen, not all at once. (Begins to laugh). We both really felt like something is truly missing in our lives, and it's the Lord. We want change and we need GOD for that. We are willing to try. We do want our marriage to work, not just for us, but for our sons. There is a church a few blocks from us. We can join when we get back home. What is it to gain the whole world and lose our soul? Hell is truly not our home.

Howard: Yes, we are willing to let GOD change us. I love my wife and I don't want to lose her, or the boys. I want change and I know only GOD can do it. We have to be living examples for our boys.

Danielle: I agree.

Narrator: They both hug each other very tight.

Howard: We also want to share our testimony with those that are going through as well, so we can impact lives too. You know, Joe. We gave you guys a hard time in the beginning. We just want to say we are sorry for being difficult. We know you and your wife was just trying to help. I see why the people left you both this beautiful place of love! We can feel the present of GOD here after we stopped fighting with HIM. Thank you both so much for your love and willingness to help us. (Turns and looks at Danielle) Right, baby?

Danielle: Yes, baby. That's right. How do we get saved if you don't mind me asking?

Joe: Well, all you have to do is repent. Ask Jesus for forgiveness and accept Him as your Lord and Savior. Believe in your heart that Jesus died and was risen by GOD on the third day. That He is the Son of GOD and you are saved! Pray and ask GOD to direct you to a church where you guys can worship and get training in the Word of GOD. Make sure, you also study in your own time. You both are now a new creature in Jesus Christ. Here is a scripture for you both if you are not sure that you are changed. 1 Corinthians 12:27.

Howard: Can you pray for us after we receive the Lord, Jesus Christ? We are ready to let go. We do accept and we believe as well.

Joe: Yes, we can pray for the both of you.

Narrator: They all hold hands and Joe begins to pray. The spirit of the Lord was in theroom. The four of them rejoiced in such a mighty way! The prayer ended.

Danielle: I know we are due to leave Sunday, but we would love to leave Saturday morning. We miss the boys, and we would like to start our journey. We want to go meet the pastor at the church across town if that's ok. I know this is going to be an amazing journey for the four of us. The boys will see the Lord in us and will one day want to serve as well.

Narrator: The conference is over. Danielle and Howard go to their room to pack and get ready to leave Saturday morning for home. Constance and Joe smiling and looking up to GOD saying, 'you did it again.' We helped another soul, and there are still others here to be helped. Well, our work is never done. The night had gone by and it is now Saturday morning. Howard and Danielle's cab is waiting outside for them. Everyone says their goodbyes and they head out to the airport to begin their new journey. See, no matter what the devil means for bad, GOD will truly use it for His good. 'No weapon formed against you shall prosper and every tongue which rises against you in judgment you shall condemn.' ISAIAH 54:17. Be bless everyone.

The End